THE**COUNTERPOINT**
GUITARMETHOD

Master Cadences, Figured Bass, Species Counterpoint, Baroque Voice Leading & More

JACK**HANDYSIDE**

FUNDAMENTAL**CHANGES**

The Counterpoint Guitar Method

Master Cadences, Figured Bass, Species Counterpoint, Baroque Voice Leading & More

ISBN: 978-1-78933-468-5

Published by **www.fundamental-changes.com**

Copyright © 2025 Jack Handyside

Edited by Joseph Alexander

www.fundamental-changes.com

Instagram: **FundamentalChanges**

For over 350 Free Guitar Lessons with Videos Check Out

www.fundamental-changes.com

Cover Image Copyright: Shutterstock

Author Image Used by kind permission of Lewis Gilchrist

Contents

Introduction

Counterpoint is the art of weaving two or more melodic ideas together to create rich, expressive polyphonic music. It is a core principle of composition that brings depth, interaction, and movement to melodies.

The study of counterpoint is often linked to the classical piano and vocal traditions of the Renaissance and Baroque periods, where many of its key innovations emerged. However, counterpoint extends far beyond Western classical music. It is a universal technique found in jazz, rock, folk, and even contemporary pop, all of which draw inspiration from its intricate interplay of voices.

For many guitarists, counterpoint can feel like an unfamiliar and daunting concept. Traditionally regarded as a skill for pianists and composers, many approaches focus on techniques that don't easily translate to the guitar. Yet, the guitar is an inherently versatile and rebellious instrument, capable of defying convention and embracing new possibilities. Its unique tuning and fingering systems present both challenges and opportunities for exploring counterpoint in fresh and exciting ways.

My fascination with counterpoint began when I first heard the music of jazz pianist Keith Jarrett. His ability to interweave melodies with effortless fluidity inspired me to apply similar ideas to the guitar. After years of study and experimentation in classical and jazz settings, I have come to see counterpoint as a vast, largely unexplored landscape on the guitar and a place where new sounds and ideas await discovery.

Many of my musical colleagues and students have encouraged me to write this book, as they know the challenges guitarists face when trying to learn counterpoint. Unlike other instruments, accessible educational material is scarce, making it difficult for guitarists to bridge the gap between theory and practical application. With this book, I hope to change that.

Counterpoint is often perceived as an academic pursuit, hidden behind complex terminology and confined to traditional conservatories. This book is designed to break down those barriers. It teaches counterpoint in a clear, engaging, and practical way, helping guitarists to reimagine chord progressions, songwriting, and improvisation. Through this approach, I hope to offer a fresh perspective on the fretboard and help you to unlock the full creative potential of your guitar.

Jack

Get the Audio

The audio files for this book are available to download for free from www.fundamental-changes.com. The link is in the top right-hand corner. Click on the "Guitar" link then simply select this book title from the drop-down menu and follow the instructions to get the audio.

We recommend that you download the files directly to your computer (not to your tablet or phone) and extract them there before adding them to your media library. If you encounter any difficulty, we provide technical support within 24 hours via the contact form.

Join our free Facebook Community of Cool Musicians

www.facebook.com/groups/fundamentalguitar

Tag us for a share on Instagram: FundamentalChanges

How To Use This Book

This is your guidebook to the exciting world of counterpoint. It teaches the foundational principles you need, yet develops creativity and freedom in your musical expression. As you build a solid grasp of the core concepts, you will gain the confidence to integrate counterpoint naturally into your playing.

Many musicians understand harmony through triads and chord progressions, but these concepts are relatively modern. Chords are simply a shorthand for a much older way of thinking about music. Within every pop, country, jazz, and blues chord progression lies a deeper foundation of melodic movement and voice-leading principles. This is the essence of counterpoint.

You will combine two key methods to deepen your understanding of harmony and melody: *figured bass* teaches you how to harmonise basslines, while *counterpoint* focuses on constructing melodies and countermelodies. Together, they offer a well-rounded and practical approach to counterpoint on the guitar.

Start at the beginning, even if you are an advanced player eager to explore later chapters. Mastering the basics of *species counterpoint* will make advanced techniques far more rewarding. You will also discover how understanding the rules allows you to break them creatively for better musical results.

What is the Species Counterpoint Method?

Species counterpoint, developed by Johann Joseph Fux in *Gradus ad Parnassum* (1725), teaches how to write independent melodies while managing consonance and dissonance effectively. While species counterpoint is excellent for learning the fundamentals, the later species can be too rigid for practical composition. By interspersing the first two species exercises with figured bass, you will find a more flexible and creative approach to understanding counterpoint and its role within harmony.

Why Study the Baroque Period?

The Baroque era (1600–1750) gave us *functional harmony* – a system of chord progressions, tonality, modulation, and dissonance that continues to shape music today. Whatever style of music you play, these Baroque techniques will deepen your understanding of counterpoint and its musical applications.

Why Do Intervals Matter?

Counterpoint is the study of how multiple melodies interact, and intervals are the most effective way to measure these relationships. Modern music education often relies on chord analysis to describe contrapuntal music, but this can obscure the details of voice-leading and individual melodic movement. For example, labelling Bach's music with chord symbols alone fails to capture the depth of his contrapuntal writing. To fully understand counterpoint, it is essential to focus on intervals and how they shape the interaction between melody and harmony.

How Should I Practice the Material in This Book?

Compose regularly, even if it is just a small amount each day. Each chapter builds on the previous one, so take time to complete the exercises in various ways before moving forward.

Creativity is key, so experiment with the concepts and see where they lead.

Chapter One – First Species Counterpoint

Think back to your first guitar lessons. Your teacher likely introduced basic chord shapes and a scale or two, but the deeper connections between triads, scales, and intervals may not have been explained until years later, if at all. This is the typical experience for many guitarists as they learn concepts in isolation without understanding their context or why certain chords and progressions sound pleasing.

Modern music education tends to separate melody and harmony, making older concepts like intervals and voice leading more difficult to grasp. To understand counterpoint fully, it is essential to focus on intervals rather than chords or triads and re-examine our pre-conceived "modern" ideas about the fundamental principles of music.

First Species Counterpoint

First species counterpoint teaches you how to write two-part music (two independent melodies) played one note against another in identical rhythms. Although this may seem simple, it provides the perfect foundation for learning counterpoint and using consonance effectively. By studying first species, you will learn to create two independent melodies that harmonise beautifully.

First Species Checklist

When harmonising a first species exercise, only consonant intervals may be used. These fall into two categories:

- **Perfect consonance:** Octaves, fifths, and unisons
- **Imperfect consonance:** Thirds and sixths

There are six key principles to follow:

1. Begin on a Perfect Consonance: The counterpoint should start with an octave. A fifth is acceptable but less common.

2. Dissonant Intervals Are Not Allowed: Avoid seconds, fourths, and sevenths.

3. Avoid *Consecutive* Perfect Consonances: Parallel (successive) fifths and octaves should be avoided, as they weaken melodic independence.

4. Vary Melodic Motion Throughout: Melodies should primarily move in contrary motion (different directions), though similar and parallel motion are acceptable in moderation.

5. End with Contrary Motion: The final cadence *must* use contrary motion, where the melodies move in opposite directions.

6. Avoid Repetition: Repeating a note will make the melody static and uninteresting.

All our species exercises are built on a fixed bassline known as the *cantus firmus* (Latin for "fixed melody"), which is written in whole notes per bar and shown below.

Example 1a:

How to Write a Memorable Melody

The first species checklist provides a solid foundation for writing a countermelody, but these additional tips will help bring your lines to life.

Melodies with a clear contour are naturally more engaging. This helps the counterpoint flow smoothly while avoiding static or repetitive motion.

Using high notes sparingly helps maintain the melodic shape and creates a sense of phrasing. If a peak note is repeated too often, it weakens the melodic direction.

The following examples show first species counterpoint writing that follows these tips.

In the first example, our counterpoint begins with an octave and moves in the opposite direction to the bassline. This satisfying example ends with both melodies resolving in the final bar in opposite directions.

Example 1b:

Here's a more liberal interpretation of Fux's rules that opens with a fifth. It shows how consecutive thirds add variety and maintain the melodic independence of both melodies.

Example 1c:

The next idea has a particularly satisfying balance as there's clear direction, a variety of intervals and melodic shape.

Example 1d:

Each example is singable and easy to identify alongside the bassline.

Common Errors

Being able to self-correct your work will make you a better counterpoint writer. Some errors are very easy to spot but others require a closer look. Here are the most common errors to watch out for:

- Parallel (successive) fifths and octaves weaken the melodic independence of both parts

- Repetition of a single pitch reduces movement and interest

- Excessive numbers of large leaps can sound disjointed

- Weak cadences do not give a satisfying ending

- Moving in tritones creates unnecessary tension

The next few examples will demonstrate some common pitfalls and explain why they don't work so well.

Parallel fifths and octaves are easier to spot on the guitar than on the piano. Picture a power chord shape and you will quickly recognise the parallel fifths below.

Example 1e:

Voice-leading emphasises smooth, stepwise melodic motion that avoids large leaps that create difficult-to-sing melodies. This idea shows a melody with too many leaps.

Example 1f:

When approaching perfect fifths and octaves, it is best to use contrary motion. Example 1g shows how using similar motion weakens the approach to a fifth.

Example 1g:

This idea includes tritone intervals. Tritones are a harsh dissonance created by a melody moving up or down a diminished fifth interval (like B to F).

Example 1h:

Your Turn

It's time to begin composing your own counterpoint ideas. Once you start writing, things will fall into place. These basslines are here for you to add countermelodies above and there are endless ways to approach each one. Use the checklist at the beginning of the chapter to review your work as you go. With a bit of practice, your ears will naturally start to recognise good counterpoint.

Example 1i:

Example 1j:

Chapter Two – Introducing Figured Bass

Figured bass is a Baroque shorthand system for notating how to harmonise basslines and helps us explore the major scale more creatively. It uses numbers to indicate which intervals to play above a bass note.

Like lead sheets in jazz or pop, it serves as a cheat sheet for creating harmonies in Baroque music.

Connecting Counterpoint to Figured Bass

Like first species counterpoint, figured bass avoids parallel fifths and octaves to keep melodies independent and harmonies interesting. While it's easy to look at figured bass as a system for creating chords, it's far more important to realise that each note is an independent melody.

Chords in the Baroque Era

Instead of naming chords like C major or G minor, Baroque musicians stacked intervals such as thirds and fifths above a written bass note to indirectly create chords. These are indicated by numbers written above or below the stave. For example, if the numbers 3 and 5 are written above a bass note, the player should play the bass note and the notes a third and a fifth above.

Thirds are the most common interval to harmonise a bassline and this example shows how we could use them to harmonise a C Major scale bassline. Notice that the number 3 above the notation tells us to play a single third above the bassline.

Example 2a:

Figured bass notation normally adds two consonant intervals above a bass note. These are either:

• Perfect Intervals (fifths or octaves) which create musical stability

• Imperfect Intervals (thirds or sixths) that add gentle, yet pleasant tension and movement

Figured Bass Notation

The three most common figures for harmonising are as follows:

• **5-3**: Play the intervals of a fifth and a third above the bass

• **6-3**: Play the intervals of a sixth and a third above the bass

• **6-4**: Play the intervals of a sixth and a fourth above the bass

It can be helpful to relate these figures to modern chord language. 5-3 is a root position triad, 6-3 is a first inversion triad, and 6-4 is a second inversion triad. Here are these three different figures played over a C bass note.

Example 2b:

This example shows an alternative approach using the same intervals. Notice that the intervals are the same, they're simply played in different octaves.

Example 2c:

In the next two examples the C Major scale is harmonised using a mix of figures. Notice that 5-3 chords most commonly occur on the first and fifth degrees of the scale.

Example 2d:

Good voice-leading is created when the melody notes move by step as much as possible.

Example 2e:

6-4 figures are the least common as the slightly dissonant fourth stands out. They're mainly used to create passing chord movements, but more on this later.

Example 2f:

Example 2g:

Working with Basslines

Unlike these exercises, real basslines often feature leaps and more varied motion. Smooth voice-leading in the top voice is still necessary but the middle voice is usually given greater melodic freedom. Here's the bassline that'll be used in the following examples.

Example 2h:

This idea shows one possibility for harmonising the bassline. If you spotted the 8-5-3, don't be alarmed! It's always fine to add the octave to the 5-3 chord for a clear resolution and more voice-leading possibilities.

Example 2i:

Here's another way to harmonise the bassline by rearranging the same intervals.

Example 2j:

These two examples use the same bassline with different figured bass to create alternative harmonies.

Example 2k:

Here, the top line moves in the opposite direction to the bass, which creates an interesting counterpoint.

Example 2l:

Descending Basslines and Augmented Sixths

As Baroque music developed, more expressive harmony was born with concepts like the augmented sixth chord adding richness and smooth voice-leading to descending scales.

An augmented sixth is a sixth that's raised by a semi-tone and often appears on the sixth degree of a descending scale. For example, in C Major, raising the sixth of the A minor chord (F to F#) creates a strong pull toward the fifth degree (G), making the transition to the 5-3 smoother and more satisfying.

The next two ideas show descending C Major scales with raised sixths (F#).

Example 2m:

Example 2n:

The next two examples use augmented sixth chords to create smooth chromatic movement (F – F# – G) in the middle voices when leading to dominant 5-3 chord.

Example 2o:

Example 2p:

Try It Yourself

Practicing figured bass in different keys is a great way to build confidence. Once you feel comfortable with harmonising the following ideas, move on to real basslines, as they are much more practical and enjoyable to work with.

Example 2q:

When the bass moves quickly it is best to sustain the harmony from the previous chord. This simplifies the arrangement and helps to maintain a smooth flow in the bassline.

Example 2r:

Example 2s:

Key change! This bassline is in the key of G major.

Example 2t:

Finally, here's a fresh bassline in E Major for you to harmonise.

Example 2u:

Now try writing your own basslines and adding figured bass notation to harmonise them.

Chapter Three – Second Species Counterpoint

Second species counterpoint adds variety to your melodies by playing two notes against one and using passing tones to introduce dissonance. This is a major step toward understanding cadences, advanced figured bass harmony, and rhythmic development. Second species counterpoint is an essential foundation of Baroque music and mastering the skills in this chapter will unlock tools for crafting more dynamic chord progressions and melodies.

Baroque musicians carefully managed dissonance by placing it on weak beats (two, three or four) and resolving the tension onto strong beats.

Dissonance occurs when two notes clash, creating tension instead of harmony. Unlike consonant intervals (thirds, fifths, and sixths), which sound pleasant and stable, dissonant intervals add excitement and movement to a melody. The three dissonant intervals are seconds, fourths and sevenths.

Passing tones are dissonant notes that function as musical "bridges" that smoothly connect two consonant notes. They are mostly found in descending melodies that move stepwise.

This bassline will be used in all examples in this chapter.

Example 3a:

In the following example, a 3-2 passing tone is created when the third (E) moves to a dissonant second (D) on the weak beat. It will usually resolve to C.

Example 3b:

This 8-7 passing tone occurs when the octave (C) moves down to a dissonant seventh (B). It will usually resolve to A.

Example 3c:

The 5-4 passing tone is another common type. This occurs when the fifth (G) moves down to a dissonant fourth (F). It will usually resolve to E.

Example 3d:

The 6-5 passing tone is unique as, unlike the others, it does not contain a dissonant interval and shows us that passing tones don't always have to be dissonant. It starts with the sixth (A), moves to the fifth (G), and typically resolves to F.

Example 3e:

The following examples demonstrate these counterpoint techniques and how to maintain smooth voice-leading and effective dissonance resolution.

This example features smooth stepwise movement and contrary motion between bars six and seven. While most dissonances resolve downward, one instance of upward motion resolves a fourth in bar six.

Example 3f:

Now notice how the dissonance in bar five resolves upward. This technique, called a neighbour tone, momentarily moves away from a consonant note before returning (C – B – C) to create a sense of movement.

Example 3g:

This idea contains a large leap of a fifth in bar five. While leaps can disrupt smooth melodic flow, descending stepwise motion after the leap fills the gap, making the melody more fluid.

Example 3h:

A *cambiata* is a melodic device where a leap (such as a third) is later filled in by the missing note. In the following example, bars six and seven show a cambiata, where the G fills the gap created by the leap from A to F in bar six.

Example 3i:

This final example features a combination of large leaps, neighbour tones, and an interesting melodic shape.

Example 3j:

Great job! You have now learned the key techniques of second species counterpoint. This builds on what you learned in first species, but with some important new rules:

- The counterpoint melody in second species should be on beat 3 to give it more independence from the bass

- Place dissonance on the weak beats only (2, 3, or 4 but never 1)

- Always resolve dissonant notes stepwise, either up or down

Second species exercises are straightforward if you follow stepwise motion and use passing tones correctly. However, some common mistakes can still occur. Most importantly, parallel octaves and fifths are still forbidden. Even when these consonant intervals appear on a weak beat, they can cause unexpected clashes in your counterpoint.

The next examples highlight common mistakes. Parallel fifths can be difficult to spot. In the following example, they occur on the weak beat of bar four and the strong beat of bar five.

Example 3k:

An uncompensated leap is a sudden, unprepared large jump in the melody. In this example, notice the leap in bar three, consecutive leaps in bars 3-4, and a non-permitted ninth leap in bars 6-7.

Example 3l:

Strong beat dissonances occur when dissonant intervals appear on beat one. This is one of the easiest mistakes to identify. In the following example, note the second on the strong beat in bar four, the seventh in bar six, and the fourth in bar eight.

Example 3m:

The next example illustrates three common dissonance mistakes. 1) Unresolved dissonance: dissonant notes must be resolved stepwise (bar two). 2) Unprepared dissonance: dissonant notes should be approached stepwise (bar five). 3) Tritones: avoid diminished fifth leaps, which create harsh clashes (bar seven into eight).

Example 3n:

If a dissonance appears on a weak beat without preparation, it creates an unresolvable tension. In the following example, notice how fourths appear on both strong and weak beats without proper preparation.

Example 3o:

Here are four new basslines for you to harmonise using second species counterpoint. Don't be afraid to get creative as there are many ways to harmonise each one. Write a melody that sounds natural and musical, rather than just "technically" correct. Play through them to ensure they feel satisfying and expressive.

Example 3p:

Example 3q:

Example 3r:

Example 3s:

Chapter Four – Minor Key Harmony

Until now, we have focused on major keys, but minor key harmony brings its own unique challenges and possibilities. In the Baroque period, composers and theorists could not quite agree on how to handle the sixth and seventh degrees of the minor scale, which led to three main variations. After much debate, the *classical melodic minor* scale emerged as the preferred choice for shaping harmony and melody.

What's With All the Scales?

The notation below shows the most common minor scales of the Baroque era. They are essentially the same scale albeit with different sixth and seventh degrees.

C Natural Minor: R–2–b3–4–5–b6–b7 = C D Eb F G Ab Bb

C Melodic Minor: R–2–b3–4–5–6–7 = C D Eb F G A B

C Harmonic Minor: R–2–b3–4–5–b6–7 = C D Eb F G Ab B

Example 4a:

The classical melodic minor scale balances two minor scales in a way that makes melodic writing more fluid. When ascending, we play the melodic minor version with a raised sixth and seventh that creates a strong pull toward resolution. When descending, we play the natural minor version, as the flattened sixth and seventh create a smoother motion.

Ascending (Melodic Minor): R–2–b3–4–5–6–7–R

Descending (Natural Minor): R–b7–b6–5–4–b3–2–R

Example 4b:

So, when writing a C Minor melody that ascends, use the raised sixth and seventh (A, B) for a stronger resolution. When writing a C Minor melody that descends, use the flattened sixth and seventh (Ab, Bb) for smoother motion. This example demonstrates these principles with 5-3 and 6-3 figurations over an ascending bassline.

Example 4c:

When writing counterpoint, a descending bassline often uses the natural minor scale (flattened sixth and seventh) as above. However the melody can still use notes from the ascending version of the melodic minor scale like B natural.

Example 4d:

Of course, real basslines are rarely this predictable and often change direction. The final bar of the next example includes an A–B–C movement from the C Melodic Minor scale to close the progression.

Example 4e:

Here's one way to harmonise the bassline from the previous example.

Example 4f:

The flexibility of the melodic minor's sixths and sevenths gave composers greater freedom when writing bass and melody lines. In the next example, taken from Bach's *Bourrée in E Minor* (transposed to C Minor), you can see this concept at play in bar three.

Example 4g:

Arcangelo Corelli: A "Baroque" Star

Born 32 years before Bach, Arcangelo Corelli was regarded as one of the greatest composers of his time. His music is known for its clarity and elegance, making it a perfect reference for Baroque harmony and counterpoint. The following excerpt from his *Sarabande in D Minor* beautifully illustrates a D Melodic Minor idea in two-voice counterpoint.

Example 4h:

The next example, transposed from Corelli's *Sarabande in E Minor, Op. 5, No. 8*, shows a busier bassline that uses A Melodic Minor for its harmonisations. Notice how bar six uses both flattened and raised sevenths in the bass for added interest but avoids raised sixths (F#), making full use of A Natural Minor.

Example 4i:

J.S. Bach, often seen as the central figure of Baroque music, redefined counterpoint in a way that pushed the boundaries of melody and harmony. Though some considered his work overly intricate and dissonant, his approach expanded the expressive potential of Baroque composition. However, for learning the fundamentals of counterpoint, composers like Telemann, Corelli, and Handel provide clearer and more conventional examples.

To see how Bach approached minor harmony, look at the next example, a transcription of *BWV 285*. Like Corelli, Bach uses the C Melodic Minor scale. The B natural serves as a leading tone to C, while the flattened sixth (Ab) adds a darker, melancholic quality.

Example 4j:

Now it's your turn to harmonise some basslines. Accidentals for raised or flattened sixths and sevenths have been removed, so it is up to you to decide how you want to apply the classical melodic minor. Trust your ear and experiment with different possibilities. Note that consecutive 5-3 chords are common in minor keys and the fifth and first degrees (G and C) naturally resolve this way.

Example 4k:

Example 4l:

Example 4m:

Bach used chorales to teach students how to harmonise a melody and bass using middle voices. The following exercise follows a similar approach and uses 8-5-3 and 8-6-3 figures to provide a wide range of note choices. Fill in the middle voices to complete the chorale.

Example 4n:

Chapter Five – Advanced Figured Bass

You are now you ready to add more depth to your harmonisations by adding *chordal dissonance*. By incorporating dissonant intervals into figured bass voicings, you will learn how to resolve these tensions smoothly, unlocking richer harmonies, better voice leading, and more expressive melodies.

This is a challenging chapter, but stick with it as the rewards are significant. Understanding chordal dissonance will deepen your appreciation of Bach and other great composers.

The three dissonant intervals are the second (or ninth), the fourth, and the seventh, and they create four key chordal dissonances when combined with figured bass:

- **7-5-3** (a 5-3 chord with an added seventh)

- **6-5-3** (a 6-3 chord with an added fifth)

- **6-4-3** (a 6-3 chord with an added fourth)

- **6-#4-2** (a 6-4 chord with an added second)

Here are these dissonances shown in the key of C Major and how they resolve.

Example 5a:

Rule of the Octave

Developed in Italian music schools in the early 1700s, the Rule of the Octave (R.O.) is a method for harmonising ascending and descending bass scales with standard chord progressions. It provides a practical way to understand voice leading, figured bass, and chordal dissonance. Rather than prescribing fixed chords, R.O. offers flexible harmonic options that help musicians learn how to resolve dissonance naturally within a tonal framework. In practice, this means playing a bass scale while applying a specific set of chords that change depending on the direction of motion, either ascending or descending.

At first, the R.O. might just seem like a collection of chords, but its purpose is to teach you how dissonance is resolved. While its chord movements resemble V–I resolutions, seeing these in terms of intervals rather than chord movements allows you to recognise and resolve dissonance more fluently.

Originally created for keyboard instruments, R.O. can be challenging to apply on the guitar due to its closely fingered intervals like sixths and fifths. To make it more accessible, we learn it in three different positions:

Position 1: The *root* is the highest note.

Position 2: The *third* is the highest note.

Position 3: The *fifth* is the highest note.

This example shows a simplified version of R.O. and harmonises the G Major scale with basic figures.

Example 5b:

Now look at the first position of R.O., where the root is the highest melody note.

Example 5c:

Here's position 2 where the third is the highest note. Notice how 6-#4-2 always resolves to 6-3.

Example 5d:

Here's position 3, where the fifth is the highest note. Pay attention to the augmented #6 (C#) in bar six.

Example 5e:

In minor keys there's a key difference in the way we handle the bassline. When ascending we use the melodic minor scale but when descending we use the natural minor scale. This example shows position 1 of R.O. in G Minor.

Example 5f:

This example in position 2 uses an alternative bass voicing an octave higher.

Example 5g:

Position 3 completes the minor version of R.O.

Example 5h:

Let's look at R.O. in the key of C Major, starting with position 1.

Example 5i:

The next example shows position 2.

Example 5j:

Finally, position 3.

Example 5k:

Now for the C Minor positions, starting with position 1.

Example 5l:

Here's position 2.

Example 5m:

Finally, position 3.

Example 5n:

The Rule of the Octave (R.O.) is a great tool for harmonising stepwise basslines, but real music doesn't follow it from start to finish. Instead, composers used small sections of it to shape phrases and resolve dissonance. Rather than seeing R.O. as a rigid sequence, it's more useful to break it into smaller formulas, each showing how to resolve dissonance step by step.

R.O. harmonises full ascending and descending scales, but real basslines change direction frequently. This makes it more practical to apply R.O. in short segments rather than as a continuous pattern. Like punctuation in a sentence, cadences create moments of rest where the harmony stabilises before continuing. Within R.O., certain points act as mini cadences, marking phrase endings.

- The tonic (I) appears at the beginning and end, providing resolution

- The dominant (V) creates tension, often appearing as a 5-3 chord resolving to the tonic

- Chords like 6-3 and 6-4-2 add movement, guiding the harmony toward the next stable 5-3 chord

By dividing R.O. into four sections, with 5-3 chords as key resting points, the harmonic structure becomes clearer, revealing four mini cadences within the sequence. The following example illustrates this breakdown.

Example 50:

Chapter Six – Suspensions

Suspensions are dissonant notes that linger briefly before resolving. They build tension and encourage forward motion to prevent melodies from becoming static.

The three most common types of suspension in the top voice are 4-3, 7-6 and 9-8, and when creating a suspension there are three distinct stages: *preparation*, *dissonance* and *resolution*. Resolution always occurs with a downward movement in pitch.

• If the melody holds and the bass moves, it is a melody suspension

• If the bass holds and the melody moves, it is a bass suspension

This example shows a 4-3 suspension, where C is prepared in the first chord, sustained over the next bass note (G) to create a dissonance of a fourth, and then resolves downward to B in beat 4.

Example 6a:

4-3 suspensions naturally occur in 6-5-3 and 6-4-3 chords. When a suspension starts on a strong beat, it creates an accented dissonance which has a stronger effect than when it is created as a tied note.

Example 6b:

This idea shows both types of suspension. Bar one features a 4-3 suspension created by the bass movement, while the bar two contains a suspension created by the melody. 4-3 suspensions are most often played over scale degrees I, III, and V.

Example 6c:

Suspension *chains* occur when multiple suspensions are linked together. The key to constructing them lies in the starting interval, which determines how the bass moves to continue the suspension in the upper melody.

4-3 suspensions typically resolve to 5-3, with the bass moving in descending fourths or rising fifths. This example shows how a suspension chain can disguise parallel octaves or fifths by delaying resolution.

Example 6d:

Starting on a different starting interval affects the entire movement. Here, the chain begins with a third that encourages a stepwise descending bassline.

Example 6e:

In the next variation, the suspension chain starts with a fifth with added thirds on strong beats for richer harmony.

Example 6f:

7-6 suspensions are highly flexible and can be used in both ascending and descending forms. The seventh dissonance can be placed on the strong beat to imply a 7-5-3 chord moving to a 6-3. This first suspension chain begins with an octave and uses a descending stepwise bass.

Example 6g:

Now look at how the suspension behaves when starting from the seventh. The descending stepwise bassline supports the motion.

Example 6h:

Ascending basslines can also work alongside 7-6 suspensions when beginning from the octave.

Example 6i:

Here, the suspension chain starts with a third. The bassline jumps in fourths then descends stepwise, which in one of the most common ways to use this technique.

Example 6j:

The final 7-6 suspension chain starts with a fifth. This encourages the bass to jump down a third while rising by step to reset the pattern in each bar. Regardless of whether the key is major or minor, these patterns function the same way.

Example 6k:

9-8 suspensions usually appear over scale degrees I, IV, and VI and behave differently because a ninth is a compound interval (a second raised by an octave), making them trickier to prepare and resolve smoothly. This is because preparing a 9-8 suspension with an octave results in parallel octaves.

For this reason, 9-8 suspensions require three voices instead of two. Combining the ninth with a tenth eliminates the harsh sound produced when using only two voices. Here's a 9-8 suspension written in three voices, starting with a third and featuring a rising bassline.

Example 6l:

This idea begins with a fifth and includes an ascending bassline that rises by a fourth while falling stepwise from bar to bar. Don't worry if you struggle to keep both the ninth and third ringing together.

Example 6m:

This 9-8 suspension chain begins with a third and features a descending stepwise bassline that rises stepwise in each bar. It is the opposite of the ascending chain you learned above.

Example 6n:

Switching to C Minor, here's a 9-8 suspension chain in C Minor that begins with a third. The bassline descends stepwise from bar to bar while the upper voice ascends stepwise.

Example 6o:

Handel's *Minuet in G Minor* is a perfect example of how advanced figured bass and suspensions appear in real music.

Example 6p:

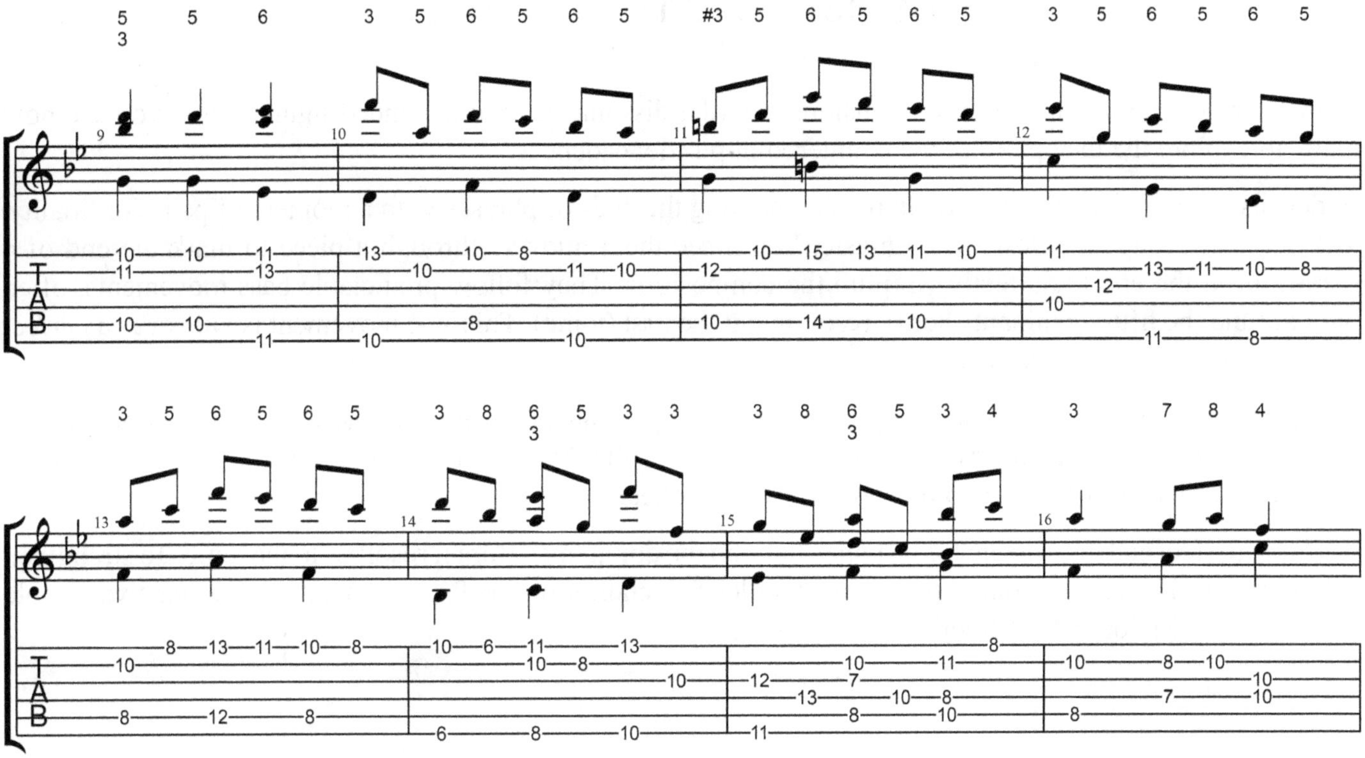
5 5 6 3 5 6 5 6 5 #3 5 6 5 6 5 3 5 6 5 6 5
3
3 5 6 5 6 5 3 8 6 5 3 3 3 8 6 5 3 4 3 7 8 4
3 3

Chapter Seven – Cadences

With your new understanding of suspensions, chordal dissonance, and advanced figured bass, you are now ready to explore the final piece of the counterpoint puzzle: cadences.

Cadences function like punctuation in music, marking the ends of phrases with a moment of pause or finality, and they help shape the flow of the music. You'll see them midway through a piece to mark the end of a phrase, or at the end to perfectly wrap up the composition. They follow predictable bass movements, often built around the fifth (dominant chord), resolving to the first (tonic). This V–I movement is known as a *perfect* cadence and is the strongest way to end a phrase.

There are three main ways to structure cadences: a *simple* cadence uses just one chord on the dominant, a *compound* cadence occurs for two beats on the dominant (often with a suspension), and the *double* cadence is created when the dominant is chord extended over four beats.

A simple perfect cadence occurs for just one chord on the dominant before it resolves to the tonic. To strengthen the sense of closure, it's common to hear parallel 5-3 chords in the final moments. Here are two simple cadences in C Major and C Minor.

Example 7a:

Simple cadences may also add sevenths on the dominant to create tension.

Example 7b:

Compound cadences extend the dominant for two beats and the second beat often contains a suspension.

The 4-3 suspension is the most common suspension in a final cadence but others can appear as well. Here are two compound cadences in C Major and C Minor.

Example 7c:

Suspensions can also be added to other beats in a compound cadence. This idea shows a 6-4 to 5-3 movement over the dominant before resolving.

Example 7d:

Composers often "recycle" cadences and the next two examples show compound cadences from Bach's *Invention No. 1* and Scarlatti's *Sonata K438*. Can you spot the similarities?

Example 7e:

Example 7f:

A double cadence extends the dominant for four beats to create a much stronger resolution and follows a formulaic approach to move through pre-planned figured bass patterns over the dominant chord. A suspended fourth is often included for additional tension. Here are all four figures over the dominant bass note.

Example 7g:

Here's another example of a double cadence played higher on the neck.

Example 7h:

Other Types of Cadences

The next example shows three perfect cadences. To add expression, it includes a cadential 6-4, a common voice-leading technique used before the dominant bass note. Cadential 6-4 chords prepare the dominant chord by adding downward motion to the melody and typically appear on the first or fifth scale degree to prolong the resolution.

Example 7i:

The Rule of the Octave teaches us that when approaching a perfect cadence by step, a 6-5 chord over the fourth degree fits naturally. The following example shows two ways to build this progression.

Example 7j:

The half cadence, also called an imperfect cadence, functions in the opposite way to the perfect cadence. Instead of resolving to the tonic, it pauses on the dominant scale degree (V). When building the cadence, the passing 6th can be used to build extra tension. In C Major, the bass descends from C to B, A, and finally, G.

Example 7k:

A deceptive cadence, also known as an evaded cadence, looks like a perfect cadence but does not resolve to the tonic. Instead, it resolves to a 5-3 chord on the sixth scale degree, shifting unexpectedly to the relative minor key. These cadences are fun for two reasons:

1. They allow smooth modulations from major to minor keys (e.g., C Major to A Minor).

2. The bassline can be altered. E.g., to create a stronger transition from C Major into A Minor, the F and G can be replaced with F# and G#, the leading tones in the A Melodic Minor scale.

As with the perfect cadence, a 6-5 chord can be used on the fourth degree.

Example 7l:

Bach's chorales are an invaluable resource for studying cadences and voice leading. The next example is a guitar transcription of *BWV 2/6*, originally written for four voices. Like all Bach chorales, it features smooth melodic movement and frequent cadences that create natural breathing points for singers.

Look out for the perfect cadences in bars four, nine, and twelve, and the imperfect cadences in bars two and seven.

Example 7m:

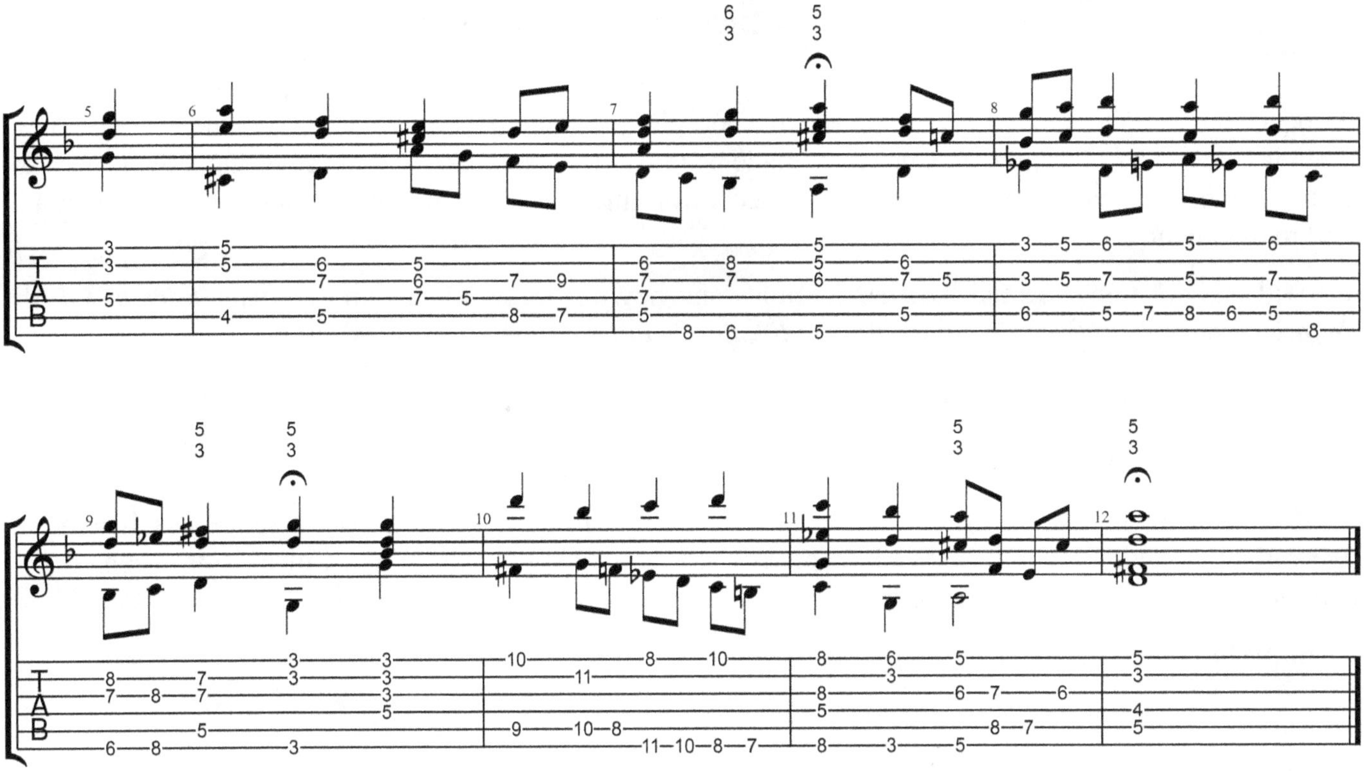
TAB

Chapter Eight – Sequences and Patterns

Baroque composers used *sequences* to transform short phrases into longer, more fluid musical passages. These formulas, known as *schemata*, provide ready-made patterns for composition and improvisation. Sequences are highly flexible and can appear anywhere in a piece, from the opening to the final cadence and can naturally lead to modulation.

We will explore four essential bassline formulas and how to develop them: the *Leaping Romanesca*, the *Stepwise Romanesca*, the *Prinner* and the *Modulating Prinner*

The Leaping Romanesca

The Romanesca, famously heard in Pachelbel's *Canon*, is one of the most recognisable sequences. It comes in two variations. This version follows a bass pattern of a descending fourth followed by a rising second that is harmonised with 5-3 chords on each bass note.

Example 8a:

This pattern naturally encourages a descending stepwise melody. Here it is harmonised with octaves and thirds to avoid parallel fifths and octaves.

Example 8b:

Here's the same pattern, but with the melody starting on the third instead of the octave.

Example 8c:

Shifting the octave over by one beat creates a double suspension chain (4-3 and 9-8) that adds tension. The following examples show two common variations of this idea.

Example 8d:

Example 8e:

Accented dissonances can be introduced to add more intensity and the next example demonstrates a 9-8 and 4-3 suspension chain. Here, the 9-4 chord can also function as a #4-2 chord in a descending sequence.

Example 8f:

To add more motion, we can fill the bass with arpeggios, which maintains the same arrival points while smoothing out the leaps.

Example 8g:

Here's the same idea starting with the third.

Example 8h:

The Stepwise Romanesca

Unlike its leaping counterpart, the stepwise Romanesca moves entirely by step. The bass follows a smooth descending line that's harmonised with alternating 5-3 and 6-3 chords. This example shows the full stepwise bassline harmonised with alternating 5-3 and 6-3 chords.

Example 8i:

A counterpoint melody can be created to ascend while the bass descends.

Example 8j:

There are many ways to harmonise a stepwise Romanesca. Here we add 5-6 suspensions to create gentle tensions before the resolutions.

Example 8k:

Breaking the harmony into arpeggios results in a more flowing sound.

Example 8l:

The Prinner

The Romanesca examples above finish around scale degree vi or v. But how do you finish the phrase?

The Prinner is a classic four-note bass descent that's used for musical closure. It follows a simple F–E–D–C pattern and works as a subtle resolution, like a mini cadence. Here's the basic template of the Prinner harmonised in thirds.

Example 8m:

Harmonising the Prinner is a straightforward process. The following example alternates 5-3 and 6-4 chords over the bass.

Example 8n:

The next three examples break the harmony into arpeggios for more fluid motion.

Example 8o:

Example 8p:

Example 8q:

For a stronger resolution, fourth leaps can be added between bass notes, reinforcing the dominant-tonic movement.

Example 8r:

Using Example 8r as a template, the next example shows how a Prinner looks with a fourth between the descending notes.

Example 8s:

The Modulating Prinner

A Modulating Prinner starts on scale degree I and falls to V instead of I (C–B–A–G in C Major). The chromatic leading tone (F#) creates the modulation by pulling toward G.

Example 8t:

By adding D before G, a fourth leap is introduced which reinforces the shift to the new key.

Example 8u:

Combining the Romanesca and Prinner

Once you have mastered the Romanesca and Prinner patterns, you can combine them to complete a phrase. The following examples show how to link the two sequences together.

Example 8v:

Example 8w:

Example 8x:

The next example uses the stepwise Romanesca for variation.

Example 8y:

Here, the first four bars use a stepwise Romanesca followed by a Prinner, while the last two bars use a modulating Prinner. Keep an eye out for the leading tone (F#).

Example 8z:

Additional Sequences and Patterns

Learning different sequences is one of the best ways to develop your counterpoint skills. At their core, sequences are built around bass movement and the melody and inner voices remain flexible, allowing for decoration and adaptation to suit different musical ideas. There are countless sequences, but the following examples highlight some of the most common patterns you can start using right away.

Stepwise Bass Patterns: The 5-6 Trick

A 5-6 sequence is a simple yet effective way to create motion while avoiding parallel fifths.

- Each strong beat lands on a 5-3 chord
- A passing 6-3 chord in between smooths the voice leading

However, since the fifth and sixth are consonant, this is not a suspension chain.

Example 8z1:

Example 8z2:

Example 8z3:

When descending, the 7-6 sequence follows the same stepwise motion downward. This pattern pairs naturally with the 5-6 sequence to create a seamless rise-and-fall effect.

Example 8z4:

Example 8z5:

Now, melodic variety can be added. The next examples demonstrate how to decorate the 5-6 and 7-6 sequences.

Example 8z6:

Example 8z7:

The 4-2 Sequence: Descending in Style

The 4-2 chord is another useful descending pattern. It always resolves downward to a 6-3 chord and frequently appears in Bach's music. These two ideas show basic versions of this sequence.

Example 8z8:

Example 8z9:

This example simplifies the movement further. It takes the first three figures and bookends the phrase with a 5-3 chord to create a perfect cadence in C.

Example 8z10:

Now, the same cadence in C Minor.

Example 8z11:

Here's how this progression may appear in a more musical form.

Example 8z12:

Leaping Bass Sequences

Leaping basslines form the foundation of many sequences. They are incredibly versatile and offer a wide range of harmonisation possibilities. Mastering these patterns requires learning how to handle leaps effectively. The most well-known leaping bass sequence is the Romanesca which was introduced earlier. Let's now look at two other essential patterns: the ascending, and descending circle of fifths.

Circle of Fifths Sequences

The circle of fifths is easy to build and harmonise. It reinforces a key and offers a smooth way to modulate. The only rule is that the bass moves by fifths, either up or down. The direction of individual notes does not matter, only the interval, and they are most commonly harmonised with 5-3 or 7-5-3 chords.

The descending circle of fifths pattern falls by a fifth then rises by a fourth, while the ascending version rises by a fifth then falls by a fourth.

This descending fifths pattern is harmonised with parallel thirds to create a simple canon in contrary motion.

Example 8z13:

Here's how the descending circle of fifths sequence appears in C Minor.

Example 8z14:

To harmonise these patterns smoothly, 7-5-3 chords can be placed on each bass note. Due to the guitar's limitations with close-voiced chords, the next example arranges these voicings for playability while maintaining good voice leading.

Example 8z15:

Here's an alternative way to harmonise the falling fifths bassline using 7-5-3 chords.

Example 8z16:

Here are two examples of the minor version of the falling sequence.

Example 8z17:

Example 8z18:

Scarlatti was a master of sequences. In *Sonata K. 287*, he integrates an ascending circle of fifths into the bass twice early on and connects each 8-5-3 chord with 4-3 suspensions in the melody. This idea highlights both instances of the ascending fifths. Can you spot them?

Example 8z19:

The best way to learn these sequences is by transposing them to different keys, using them in compositions, and improvising with them on your guitar. Writing them out for yourself will quickly reinforce what you have learned.

Chapter Nine – Modulation

Staying in one key for too long can make music feel static and repetitive, and Baroque composers maximised their simple musical ideas by moving them through different keys. Toward the end of the era, modulation and chromaticism became more common as ways to develop a piece.

To modulate effectively there are three key elements on which to focus:

• Chromaticism

• Closely related keys

• Cadences

Chromatic notes act as bridges, leading the ear smoothly into a new key. Closely related keys, which share most of their notes, make modulation feel natural and cohesive. Cadences confirm the arrival in the new key, providing a sense of resolution and stability.

A crucial part of modulation is the use of leading tones. These notes create a strong pull toward the next key and help establish it more convincingly. In C Major, the leading tone is B which resolves naturally to C. In A Minor, the raised G# produces the same effect to reinforce the shift in tonality.

The first two examples show a simple leading tone resolution, first in C Major, then in A Minor.

Example 9a:

Example 9b:

How to Modulate

The easiest type of modulations move to *closely related keys*. These are keys that share six of their seven notes. The circle of fifths diagram below shows that closely related keys are positioned directly to the left and right of your starting key, and to move between them we change just one note with an accidental.

So, to modulate from C Major to G Major (one step clockwise) we change F to F#. To modulate from C Major to F Major (one step counter-clockwise) we change B to Bb.

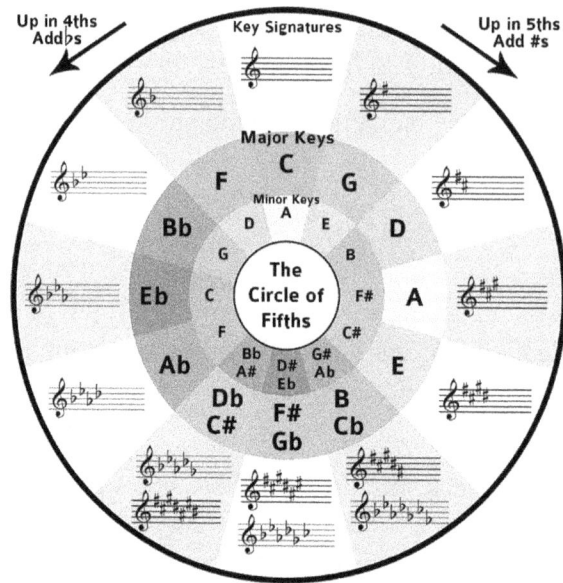

5-3 chords can be built on every scale degree, each acting as a temporary tonic or resting point. The Rule of the Octave suggests that placing a 6-5-3 chord before a 5-3 chord creates a smoother transition between harmonies, hinting at key changes without fully modulating. This allows for fluid movement within a key while subtly introducing new tonal colours. The next example demonstrates this process.

Example 9c:

A scale mutation occurs when a single note in a scale is altered to strengthen the dominant-to-tonic resolution, making modulation easier. By introducing leading tones to different scale degrees in C Major, new harmonic possibilities emerge, creating smooth pathways to closely related keys. Example 9d demonstrates this process. B moves to C major, C# moves to D minor, F# moves to G major, and lastly, G# moves to A minor.

Example 9d:

The next example attaches a 6-5-3 chord (dominant) to each chromatic leading tone, pulling the harmony into a new key. These are known as *secondary* dominant chords.

Example 9e:

This concept also applies when descending. Here's the descending scale with leading notes.

Example 9f:

This idea expands on the modulating pattern above, adding arpeggios to the melody and bass. The result is a more fluid and musical passage that naturally leads into a cadence that reinforces the key.

Example 9g:

A favourite technique of Bach's was to substitute the dominant chord with a diminished chord. This adds tension and works especially well in minor keys. In figured bass notation, this is achieved when a 6-5-3 becomes #6-5-3 to raise the sixth scale degree, turning the dominant into a diminished chord. Listen to how this technique intensifies the modulation.

Example 9h:

A final cadence strengthens the modulation and firmly establishes the new key. This passage begins in C Major and ends in A Minor with a cadence to confirm the transition.

Example 9i:

The 6-4-2 chord is a powerful way to create smooth modulations. In the Rule of the Octave, it naturally moves to 6-3 before resolving to 5-3. This descending pattern can continue through the scale, eventually leading back to the starting key. Here is this sequence in C Major.

Example 9j:

Raising the fourth (#4) introduces a leading tone, transforming the progression into a modulation. This idea shows how this approach can move through major keys. The 6-4-3 chord creates a smoother transition back to 5-3.

Example 9k:

A Simple Modulation Trick

Rather than memorising countless modulation patterns it's easier to focus on raising the leading tone of the key you want to move to, as this will naturally pull the harmony into that key.

The final example shows a sequence that moves through C Major and ends in A Minor. Can you spot the chromatic change that creates the modulation?

Example 91:

Chapter Ten – Diminution: From Chords to Melodies

With figured bass, modulation, and sequences under our belts, we now have the tools to get creative.

Diminution is the process of breaking long notes into shorter ones to add motion and intensity while outlining the harmony. Shorter notes create faster rhythms and create more movement while longer notes create space and reduce intensity. This is how Baroque composers transformed simple harmonic progressions into expressive, flowing melodies. If you have ever heard a jazz musician outlining chord changes using licks, this is the same idea. Diminutions are like Baroque jazz licks!

How to Create Diminutions

Creating diminutions is like slicing a cake. The cake itself does not change but cutting it into pieces makes it easier to share. Likewise, shorter notes spread the melody evenly while maintaining its harmonic function. As rhythms become faster, melodies gain expressiveness and intensity.

The most common ways to create diminutions are by using arpeggios (breaking chords into individual notes) and by using passing and neighbouring tones (connecting harmony notes stepwise).

For guitarists, writing in two voices is ideal for playability. Three voices can add more depth but should be used sparingly.

The next example shows a simple bassline resolving to A minor. The first three bars contain the harmonic skeleton, while the final three introduce diminutions to enhance its movement.

Example 10a:

Most examples in this book use arpeggios to create diminutions over bass sequences. Arpeggios are easy to use because every note belongs to the implied chord and can be placed freely within a bar. This idea shows how a simple 5-3 chord transforms through four stages of diminution: 1/4 notes, 1/8th notes, and 1/16th notes.

Example 10b:

This example builds on that idea by adding arpeggiated melodies over a bassline. Even though each note fits the chord, good counterpoint follows the key rule of avoiding parallel fifths and octaves on strong beats, especially between the last beat of one bar and the first beat of the next.

Example 10c:

For comparison, the next example demonstrates poor counterpoint writing. There are multiple parallel intervals. Can you spot them all?

Example 10d:

Scales notes can fill weak beats between chord tones and achieve smooth voice leading by bridging the gaps created by arpeggios. Voice leading is the glue that holds these chord tones together, shaping them into a stepwise melody.

There are two types of non-chord tones: *neighbouring tones* are steps above or below a chord tone and return to the original note. *Passing tones* move between two chord tones and continue in the same direction. The next example demonstrates both.

Example 10e:

Scales don't explicitly outline chords like arpeggios but instead connect harmonies smoothly.

Example 10f:

Passing and neighbouring tones work best on weak beats, resolving smoothly. When they appear on strong beats they create dissonance, which must be resolved carefully because this is where suspensions and accented passing tones come in.

Example 10g:

Rhythm in Diminution

Diminution controls the speed and intensity of a melody. Faster rhythms create momentum but require careful handling. Watch out for unresolved dissonances, as well as parallel fifths and octaves that can easily sneak in at the end of beats. Also be careful of consecutive accented dissonances (clashes on strong beats). Writing stepwise melodies usually prevents and fixes these issues, but when in doubt, write the intervals out. Can you spot the unresolved dissonances in the next example?

Example 10h:

Parallel fifths and octaves can be difficult to hear in fast-moving 1/16th note lines, especially in Bach's music. The following example contains some. See if you can identify them all.

Example 10i:

The final common error is back-to-back accented dissonances (dissonant notes appearing on successive beats or bars). These are often easy to hear.

Example 10j:

Combining arpeggios and scales is a fun way to get melodies flowing in different directions. The following examples present two different diminution patterns.

Example 10k:

Now in C Minor.

Example 10l:

Common Diminution Patterns

Baroque composers developed a set of diminution patterns and applied them throughout a piece, reducing errors and simplifying composition. Just like the bass patterns and sequences from earlier chapters, having a vocabulary of diminutions makes counterpoint much easier. The next examples show some useful diminution patterns over a Romanesca bassline.

Example 10m:

Example 10n:

Now, a variation including the bass.

Example 10o:

Example 10p shows Scarlatti's beautiful third movement from his *Sonata for Solo Instrument and Continuo K.90* – the perfect demonstration of diminution in action.

Example 10q strips away the passing and neighbouring tones, revealing the harmonic skeleton that Scarlatti likely started with. It shows how a simple framework can be transformed into a flowing, expressive melody through diminution.

Example 10p:

Example 10q:

Chapter Eleven – Imitation and Polyphony

Imitation occurs when a melody is repeated in another voice at the same or a different pitch. It is a powerful tool for expanding a simple theme into a full composition. Imitation also helps recycle basic ideas, exploring how they interact across multiple voices.

This technique is central to masterpieces like Bach's two and three-part inventions, Handel's fugues, and Pachelbel's canons. While this book does not cover fugues or canons in depth, mastering basic imitation will unlock countless new possibilities in your counterpoint writing.

Challenges of Polyphony on Guitar

Unlike a keyboard, where multiple melodies can be played with ease, the guitar has a limited fretboard range which makes imitation more challenging. To navigate these limitations it is best to work with only two voices, as adding more can create technical difficulties. When you're writing, starting with pen and paper helps to clarify how your melodies interact before testing them on the fretboard. Also, freely adapting your phrases to suit the guitar ensures they are playable before exploring different keys or positions.

Step 1: Write a Subject

At the start of most Bach inventions, a single melody appears on its own. This is the "subject" – the main theme that returns throughout the piece. A strong subject is often simple, with Bach frequently using scale-like ideas. Dissonances should be carefully handled, ensuring all non-chord tones are properly prepared and resolved. Stepwise motion is preferred over large leaps, as it makes imitation smoother and more fluid.

The next example shows a basic C Major subject with labelled intervals.

Example 11a:

Step 2: Write a Countersubject

The countersubject serves as a harmonic foundation, integrating figured bass principles into the imitation. This element distinguishes Bach's inventions and fugues from earlier imitative techniques. A strong countersubject follows a clear harmonic structure, with the tonic and dominant guiding the chord progression. Octaves, thirds, and sixths create stable harmonies, while the fifth should be avoided, as it can cause issues in invertible counterpoint (explained in Step 4).

The next example presents a basic countersubject that harmonises the subject.

Example 11b:

Step 3: Harmonic Expansion

The countersubject does more than support the subject, it defines the harmony, and this example introduces a middle voice to expand the harmonic framework. This strengthens the tonality, links the music to figured bass, and prepares it for invertible counterpoint. By applying these principles, simple imitation develops into a structured, tonal composition.

Example 11c:

Step 4: Double Counterpoint at the Octave

Double counterpoint occurs when two melodies interact and swap places throughout a piece. Before adding the countersubject, the subject must return at an octave above or below. This allows the countersubject to take the melody's role during the swap. This example gives a clear framework for double counterpoint at the octave, with the subject reappearing an octave lower.

Example 11d:

Step 5: Invertible Counterpoint

When the countersubject moves above or below the subject, the intervals shift, which creates invertible counterpoint. A well-constructed countersubject works in both positions, with most intervals remaining consonant. However, fifths invert to fourths, which can be unstable. Avoiding fifths in a countersubject keeps it flexible and allows for smooth inversion.

Thirds invert to sixths and remain consonant, while octaves stay the same. Seconds invert to sevenths, creating dissonance, and fourths invert to fifths, where one remains consonant and the other dissonant. Since a fifth inverts to a dissonant fourth, avoiding it when writing a countersubject prevents instability.

This example shows how thirds become sixths and create strong harmony, while fourths invert to fifths, which introduces instability.

Example 11e:

The next idea shows the subject and countersubject swapping places while maintaining good counterpoint. The first two bars show the countersubject below, and the last two bars show the countersubject above. Any sevenths, fifths, or fourths are passing tones without harmonic weight. The key intervals that shape the harmony are the thirds, sixths, and octaves.

Example 11f:

Invertible counterpoint can seem confusing at first, but there's no need to overanalyse every interval. A well-written subject and countersubject naturally avoid most issues, making the process much simpler.

Step 6: Splitting Up the Parts

The next example shows the next step to building the imitation. The subject starts on its own and in bar three the countersubject joins below. In bar five, the subject switches to the bass, and the countersubject switches to the melody.

Example 11g:

Double counterpoint at the 10th and 12th are other ways to create imitation, but they are extremely difficult, if not impossible on guitar due to the fretboard's size and hand span limitations. Thankfully, double counterpoint at the octave is sufficient for writing your own imitative pieces.

Repeating the Imitation in the Dominant Key

The next step is to transpose the subject and countersubject to the dominant key (G Major). This simple trick doubles your musical material while keeping it fresh and also helps to develop the melody. Bach uses this technique in *Invention No. 1* and many of his other contrapuntal works.

In bar seven, the subject and countersubject repeat exactly in G Major. The added leading tones (E–F#) in bar six make the transition to G Major much smoother and avoid parallels.

Example 11h:

Writing an Episode

An "episode" is a short transition between the opening imitation and the cadence. Instead of strict imitation, episodes use free counterpoint, meaning there are no strict rules, only a smooth connection to the cadence. Most episodes borrow a small piece of the subject or countersubject and turn it into a sequence that moves toward the cadence. Here, the descending line from bar two is turned into a pattern that moves scale degrees 6-5-4 down to a compound cadence. The bass voice is altered to ascend, building tension before resolving.

Example 11i:

Practice Melodies

Now, it is time to put these techniques into practice and start writing your own imitations. This is one of the most challenging exercises in the book, so don't worry if your first few attempts are not perfect. The more you write, the better your countersubjects will become. When composing a countersubject, write the intervals above each harmonised note to check for strong beat dissonances.

Example 11j:

The next melody is in A Minor. When working in minor keys, remember to raise the sixth and seventh scale degrees when ascending and lower them back to natural when descending

Example 11k:

Looking for a challenge? The next two examples have four-bar subjects, giving you more material to work with.

Example 11l:

The following example uses tied suspensions. Ensure any dissonances resolve correctly in the countersubject.

Example 11m:

This final example is a guitar transcription of the opening eight bars of Bach's *Invention No. 1 in C Major*. Here, Bach moves the subject and countersubject through C Major and into the dominant key of G Major. The rest of this short piece takes the same material through the keys of D Minor and A Minor using the techniques covered in this chapter.

Example 11n:

Chapter Twelve – Etude Collection

It's time to put everything into practice! These three etudes are designed to help you explore counterpoint, and each one applies essential concepts in different ways to help you learn how they work musically.

They are not exercises, but fully realised compositions that will challenge your technique, ear, and creativity. As you work through them, focus on how each voice moves independently while still forming a cohesive whole. Play slowly, listen carefully, and let the counterpoint guide your fingers. Most importantly, enjoy the process! This is not just a theoretical study, it is rich, expressive and rewarding way to write music.

Example 12a:

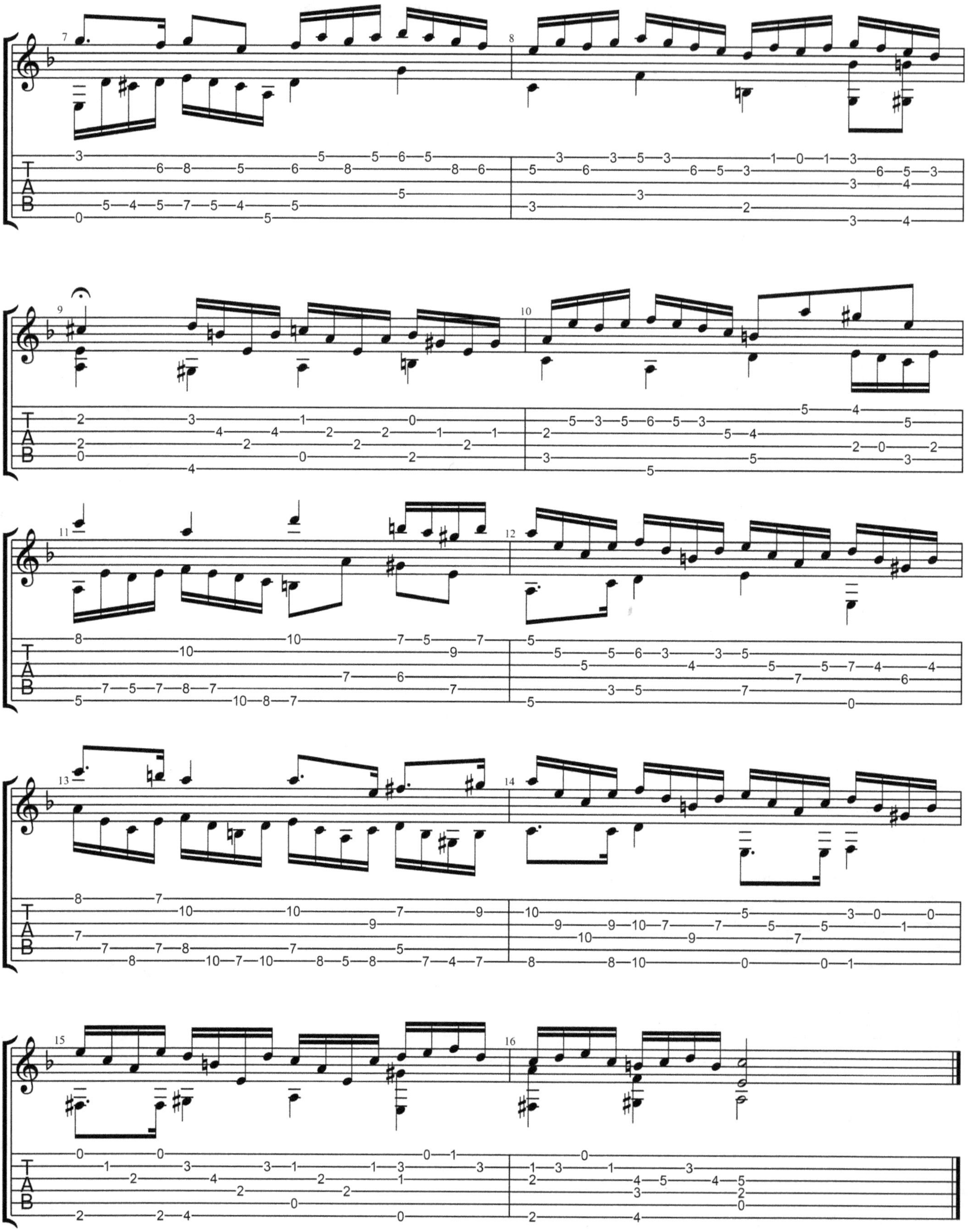

Example 12b:

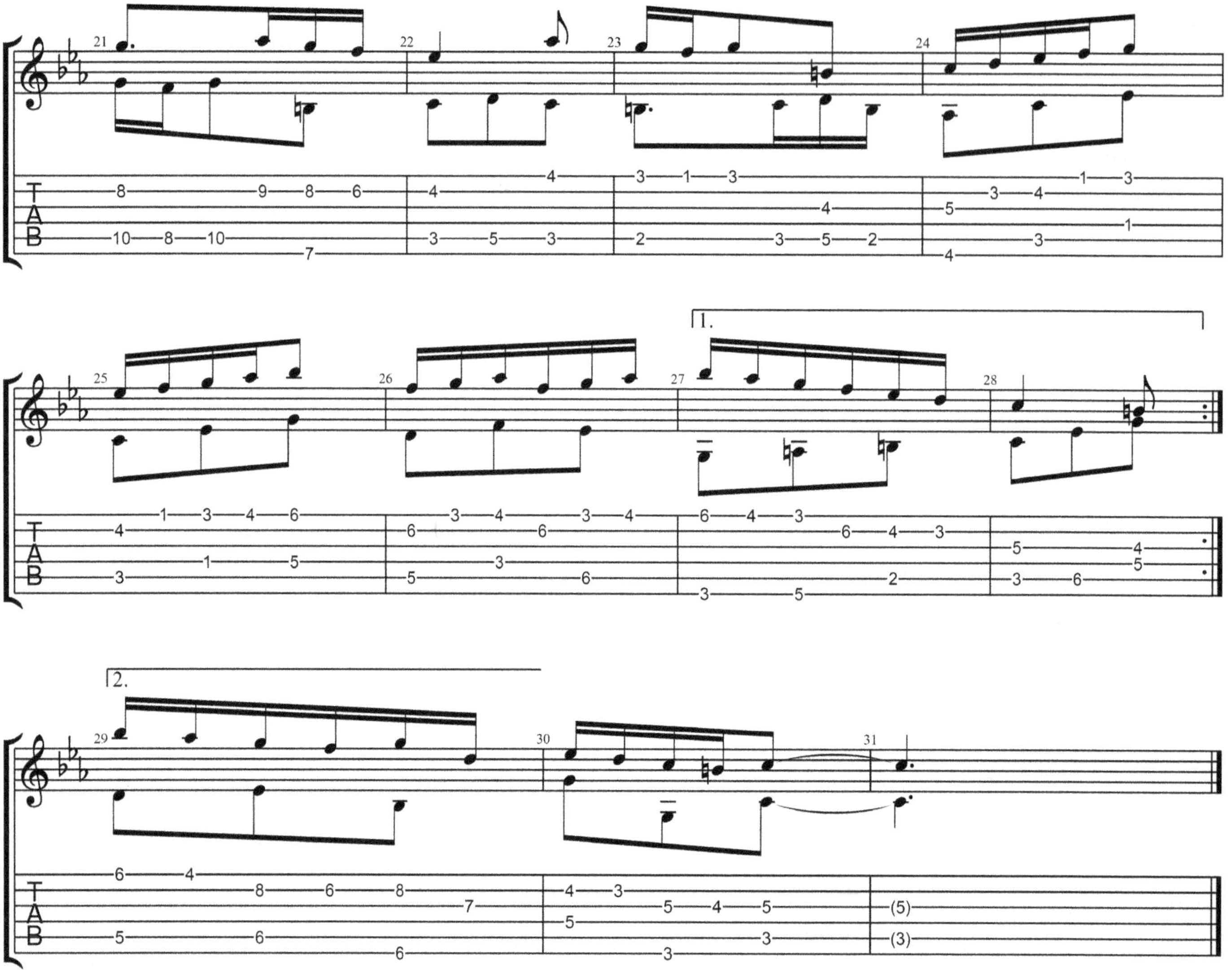

Example 12c:

Conclusion

The study of counterpoint is a lifelong journey and no matter how much you learn, there's always more to discover. This book has introduced key ideas from Baroque music and beyond, but real mastery takes time. You will need to revisit these lessons many times before everything fully clicks. This is completely normal, and your understanding will grow with practice.

Thinking in intervals can feel unnatural at first. It is a different, more structured way of approaching music, but voice leading, consonance and dissonance, and figured bass are not just relics of the past – these principles shape modern music, from jazz and film scores to rock and pop. Soon, the rules will stop feeling like restrictions and instead become tools for creativity.

All the great counterpoint composers pushed boundaries, broke rules, and invented new ones. Studying their techniques reveals how centuries of voice leading still influence the music we hear today. For guitarists, counterpoint remains an underexplored world – one that is still evolving and full of untapped potential.

Your next step is simply to write as much as possible. It's important to experiment, but above all *play*! Let these ideas shape how you hear and create music. The more you explore counterpoint, the more it will become second nature to you on guitar.

Jack Handyside

About The Author

Jack Handyside is a Scottish guitarist, composer, and educator based in the United Kingdom. As a performer, Jack is active on both the London and Birmingham jazz scenes as a sideman and session guitarist, showcasing his talent at Birmingham's prestigious Symphony Hall, Moseley Jazz Festival, London Jazz Festival, and Cheltenham Jazz Festival.

In the summer of 2024, Jack released his first EP project titled *In Cahoots* – a collection of compositions exploring the duo of alto saxophone and guitar.

Find out more at **www.jackhandysideguitar.com**

www.ingramcontent.com/pod-product-compliance
Lightning Source LLC
Chambersburg PA
CBHW081431090426
42740CB00017B/3268